HAPPILY EVER CRAFTER

ONCE UPON A FAIRY TALE CRAFT

ANNALEES LIM

Lerner Publications ◆ Minneapolis

First American edition published in 2020 by Lerner Publishing Group, Inc.

First published in Great Britain in 2018 by Wayland
Copyright © Hodder and Stoughton, 2018
All rights reserved.

Senior Commissioning Editor: Melanie Palmer
Design: Square and Circus
Illustrations: Supriya Sahai

Additional illustrations: Freepik

Lerner Publications Company
A division of Lerner Publishing Group, Inc.
241 First Avenue North
Minneapolis, MN 55401 USA

For reading levels and more information, look up this title at www.lernerbooks.com.

Main body text set in Billy Infant Regular 17/24.
Typeface provided by SparkyType.

Library of Congress Cataloging-in-Publication Data

Names: Lim, Annalees, author. | Sahai, Supriya, 1977– illustrator.
Title: Once upon a fairy tale craft / Annalees Lim ; Supriya Sahai [illustrator].
Description: Minneapolis : Lerner Publications, [2018] | Series: Happily ever crafter | Audience: Ages 7–11. | Audience: Grades 4–6. | "First published in Great Britain in 2018 by Wayland."
Identifiers: LCCN 2018050536 (print) | LCCN 2018058680 (ebook) | ISBN 9781541561953 (eb pdf) | ISBN 9781541558779 (lb : alk. paper) | ISBN 9781526307521 (pb)
Subjects: LCSH: Handicraft—Juvenile literature. | Fairy tales in art—Juvenile literature. | Children's parties—Juvenile literature. | Games—Juvenile literature. | Handicraft for children.
Classification: LCC TT160 (ebook) | LCC TT160 .L485243 2019 (print) | DDC 745.5—dc23

LC record available at https://lccn.loc.gov/2018050536

Manufactured in the United States of America
1-46266-46258-10/31/2018

SAFETY INFORMATION:
Please ask an adult for help with any activities that could be tricky, or involve cooking or handling glass. Ask adult permission when appropriate.

CONTENTS

ONCE UPON a TiMe...

Fairy tales are short stories with happily-ever-after endings, making them a perfect bedtime read! Follow the adventures of courageous knights and brave princesses as they travel through enchanted kingdoms, meeting mythical creatures along the way.

It's easy to make these stories come to life in your imagination, and you can turn them into a reality by following our simple step-by-step instructions. In this book you will find out how to transform everyday household objects into magical creations, perfect for decorating your themed parties, as gorgeous gifts for friends and family, or just to enjoy all for yourself!

With a sprinkle of fairy dust and just a bit of glue, you can make all your crafty dreams come to life. You won't have to make believe when you can make it yourself! Always ask an adult to help you before you start, especially if you are using sharp tools like scissors. Remember to cover all surfaces—this keeps them from getting messy with paint or glue. Don't forget to wash your hands when you're finished!

FACT!

The Brothers Grimm originally collected stories and folklore from all around Germany. They were the first to start writing them down and sold the first copies of *Grimms' Fairy Tales* in 1812. The stories have changed over the years to be those we recognize today, and they are still enjoyed by children all over the world.

TOP TIP

Collect things from around the house for your craft supplies. Old magazines and newspapers make great scrap paper. And don't throw away cardboard tubes, plastic containers, or old food wrappers—they can all be turned into the fantastic fairy tale crafts you will find in this book.

COSTUMES AND CHARACTERS

Dressing up is a great way to get into character and turn into the heroes and villains of your favorite stories. There are hundreds of different people and mysterious creatures you can transform into, but if you are stuck, try out these creative costume ideas for size!

MERMAID TAIL

If you can't be under the sea, this shimmery tail is the perfect way to let you swim around with your friends without getting your feet wet.

You Will Need:

- A PAIR OF OLD PANTS
- FABRIC GLUE • SCISSORS
- CARDBOARD • SHINY FABRIC
- PENCIL • PAINTBRUSH
- (OPTIONAL: WHITE CRAFT GLUE AND GLITTER)

1. Lay your pants out flat and cut off the inside seams.

2. Join the pants together again by overlapping the edges and gluing them together.

3. Cut out some U-shaped scales from your shiny fabric and stick them onto the pants using fabric glue.

TOP TIP

If you don't have any spare shiny fabric, make your own. Cover old fabric scraps with watered-down paint. Once dry, paint another layer with a mixture of PVA glue, water, and glitter.

4. Draw a tail shape onto the cardboard, then cut it out. Decorate the tail shape with more fabric before sticking it onto the bottom of the pants.

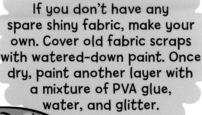

FIERY, FIERCE DRAGON

These reptile-like creatures have lots of scales, two flappy wings on their back, and a long, spiky tail. Be careful—they also breathe fire!

You Will Need:

- 2 OLD PILLOWCASES
- SCISSORS • PAINT
- PAINTBRUSH • NEWSPAPER
- SCRAP FABRIC • FABRIC GLUE

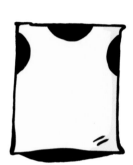

1. Use scissors to cut out neck and arm holes from one pillowcase.

2. Cut the other pillowcase in half and stick one corner to the back of the neck hole to make your hood.

3. Use the leftover pillow material to make your tail. Stick this onto the bottom of the body.

4. Place some newspaper inside the pillowcase before you paint on the scales, eyes, nose, and wings.

TOP TIP

If you have more spare fabric, cut up extra triangles and stick them on the back to make a spine of spikes.

ROAR!

5. Cut some scrap fabric into triangles. Use pale colored scraps for teeth, and use two larger pieces for the ears.

WIZARD'S CAPE

No magical wizard is complete without their trusty cape to swish while casting spells. You can decorate yours with shapes and symbols or make up a special badge so that your wizarding pals can recognize you from afar.

You Will Need:

- LARGE OLD SHIRT • RIBBON
- FABRIC GLUE • SCISSORS • PAINT
- FLAT PAINT TRAY • OLD JAR (MUST HAVE STRAIGHT, SMOOTH SIDES) • FOAM OR KITCHEN SPONGE
- MASKING TAPE • BUCKET

1. Cut the sleeves from the shirt and glue the seams together to close each hole. Use ribbon or strips from the sleeves to make the cape fastenings. Glue them to the collar and leave to dry.

3. Cut out different shapes using foam or a kitchen sponge. Glue these onto the jar.

2. Add some water to paint in a bucket. Try not to make the paint too runny. Soak the shirt until it has all been dyed. Squeeze out the excess paint and hang to dry.

4. Spread paint onto the tray. Roll the jar stamp in the paint so that it is evenly spread onto the foam.

TOP TIP

You can hold the sponge pieces down with masking tape until the glue dries so that the shapes dry flat.

5. Roll the jar stamp onto the shirt, printing a continuous design. Leave to dry.

HAIRY, SCARY TROLL

In the Norwegian fairy tale "The Three Billy Goats Gruff," a scary troll lives under the bridge and gobbles up anyone who tries to cross. Will anyone manage to sneak past you without being caught?

You Will Need:
- AN OLD BEANIE HAT • SCRAP FABRIC
- FABRIC GLUE • SCISSORS
- PAPER • BLACK MARKER

2. Cut out a large circle from the scrap fabric and cut in half. Fold over and glue each piece to make a cone.

3. Leave to dry before stuffing with other pieces of scrap fabric.

1. Make two eyes from the paper and draw big black pupils on them.

4. Glue the eyes to the front and the cone horns onto the top of the beanie. Decorate with long strips of fabric, using the fabric glue to stick them in place.

ENCHANTED ACCESSORIES

If you just need something small to add that finishing touch to your costume, look no further. Remember you can choose your own colors so that your creations match your costume.

MAGIC WAND

Every fairy, witch, and warlock needs a wand to cast magic spells—you can even make it sparkle in the sunlight.

You Will Need:

- BOWL • WHITE CRAFT GLUE
- PLASTIC BAGS • TIN FOIL
- GLITTER • COOKIE CUTTER
- WOODEN SKEWER • TAPE
- PLASTIC SHEET PROTECTOR
- (OPTIONAL: CARDSTOCK)

1. Pour some craft glue into a bowl and add sparkly things into the mix. Cut up colorful bits of plastic bags, tear up tin foil scraps, or pour in some glitter.

TOP TIP

If you do not have a wooden skewer, you can just roll up some cardstock into a thin tube and tape it together instead.

2. Tape the cookie cutter onto the plastic sheet protector. Seal any gaps with more tape.

3. Pour the glue mixture into the mold. Leave to dry in a warm place. You will know it is dry when all the glue has turned see-through. This could take a few days.

4. Take the dried glue shape out of the mold and stick it onto the top of the wooden skewer.

PARTY CROWNS

Crowns are traditional headwear to show everyone who is a member of the royal family. Make these sparkly crowns and you'll be the king or queen of your castle!

You Will Need:

- CARDBOARD • SCISSORS • TAPE
- BALLOON • TISSUE PAPER • WHITE CRAFT GLUE • (OPTIONAL: NEWSPAPER, MAGAZINES, PAINT)

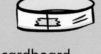

1. Make a cardboard band that fits around your head and another one that is smaller.

2. Blow up the balloon to the size of the larger cardboard band. Tape the balloon inside the band. Tape the smaller band onto the bottom of the balloon to help it stand up.

3. Tear up strips of tissue paper and stick them to the balloon to make the crown. Leave to dry in a warm place.

TOP TIP

If you do not have tissue paper you can always use newspaper and paint it, or use colorful pages from magazines.

4. Pop the balloon to remove the crown. Gently bend the crown peaks so they stand up straight. Decorate the crown.

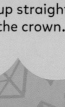

PARTY PLANNING

You have your costumes made, but don't get all dressed up with nowhere to go! Parties are a fun way to get together with your friends and celebrate birthdays or special holidays. You can pick one fairy tale as inspiration or mix them all together into one giant fable. Use these top tips to help make your party the best in all the land.

PARTY CHECKLIST

☑ **GAMES** Plan to play some fun games to get everyone in the party mood. See page 14 for some inspiration.

☑ **FOOD** Make delicious snacks and drinks that match your theme. See page 16 for some recipe ideas.

☑ **DECORATIONS** Turn ordinary rooms into enchanted realms using simple craft ideas. See page 18 for decorations or page 22 for other crafts you can make.

☑ **INVITE PEOPLE** Send out some invitations so that people remember to show up to **YOUR** party—see the next page for a template of what to say or use the craft on page 19.

GET ORGANIZED
To be the best party planner around you will need to get organized. Grab a notebook (or make the Once Upon A Time memory book on page 27) to write down all the important things to remember.

INVITATIONS

Invitations are more than just a nicely decorated piece of paper. They contain all the important information your guests need.

To: Write the name of the guest you are inviting.

Dress Code: What sort of outfits do you want your guests to wear? Fancy dress? Formal? You decide.

What: Say what sort of party your guests are being invited to.

To:

You are invited to my PARTY!

At:

RSVP:

Time:

RSVP: This means you would like your guests to tell you whether they will be coming or not. This helps you to plan how much food to make, how much space you will need, and how many party bags to make.

Time: What time will the party start and when will it end?

Where: Let your guests know where you will be holding the party.

PARTY GAMES

Get the party started with these enjoyably enchanting themed games. They are quick and easy to make but will provide you with hours of fun!

CATCH THE GENIE

The most famous tale featuring a genie is the story of Aladdin. Originally a Middle Eastern folk tale, the story tells of a poor boy who lives in China and comes across an evil sorcerer. The story has many different versions, but the genie remains a central character in all of them.

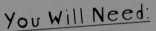
You Will Need:
- PLASTIC BAGS • SCISSORS
- TAPE • BALLOON
- PERMANENT MARKER

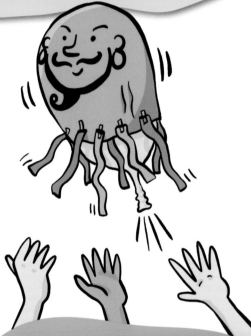

1. Cut the handles off a plastic bag.

2. Decorate the bag by adding strips of other bags, sticking them on to make some tassles.

3. Draw a face with a permanent marker so it looks like a genie.

4. Loosely tape the balloon to the inside of the bag.

HOW TO PLAY

Stand in a circle and choose one person to release the genie. That person blows up the balloon and holds it up high before releasing it. Everyone races to be the first person to catch the genie as it flies around. Make the game even more of a challenge by getting players to catch the genie with only one hand.

PRINCESS AND THE PEA TOWER

You Will Need:
- SMALL CEREAL BOX • CONSTRUCTION PAPER • SMALL CARDBOARD BOX
- KITCHEN SPONGES • SCISSORS
- PENS • GREEN TISSUE PAPER

"The Princess and the Pea" was written in 1835 by Hans Christian Anderson. It is a story about a prince who is searching for a real princess to marry. The prince hides a pea underneath a mattress as a test, since only a princess could feel the pea. This game will test you! Remember that balance is key, as well as keeping your hands steady.

HOW TO PLAY

Players take turns to roll the die. If it shows a number 1 or 2, then you have to stack that many mattresses onto the bed. If it shows a green dot, you have to place a tissue paper pea on the bed. Keep stacking the bed as tall as you can make it. The first to make it topple over loses the game.

1. Cut up small bits of paper and stick them onto the cereal box base so it looks like a bed frame.

2. Cover all sides of the cube with squares of construction paper.

3. Draw a 1, a 2, or a green dot on each side so that you have two sets of each symbol.

4. Roll up balls of green tissue paper.

5. Cut up the kitchen sponges into different shapes and sizes. You will need lots to play the game—just don't make them too much bigger than the cereal box bed base.

PARTY FOOD

Serve up platters of delicious food at your party and have a real feast. All of these recipes are easy to make and they do not need to be cooked in an oven.

GINGERBREAD HOUSE

In the story "Hansel and Gretel," two curious children go wandering into an enchanted forest and discover a gingerbread house that belongs to a wicked witch. Make your own version using chocolate and candy you love the best—no one will be able to resist your tempting treat.

1. Break one of the chocolate bars in half to make two smaller squares.

You Will Need:
- 5 BARS OF CHOCOLATE • CANDY
- ICING PENS • GINGERBREAD MEN

3. Using icing pens, decorate the gingerbread men to make Hansel and Gretel or other fairy tale characters. Stick candy onto the outside of the house and use icing to make doors, windows, and roof tiles.

2. Using the icing pens like glue, stick the two squares to the two full bars to form the base of your house. Glue together the final two bars of chocolate so they form the roof.

SAND-WITCH-ES

Witches were first drawn wearing pointed hats in early fairy tale books in the 1700s, even though they were popular headwear for lots of people in the centuries before. These "open sandwiches" are so spellbinding that they will be a hit with everyone too.

You Will Need:
- BREAD • CREAM CHEESE • HAM
- CHEESE • CHERRY TOMATOES
- SMALL KNIFE

1. Cut the slice of bread in half to make two triangles.

2. Take one triangle and cover it in a thin layer of cream cheese.

3. Cover the tip with a slice of ham. Trim to size if necessary.

4. Cover the bottom in lettuce, making the brim of the hat.

5. Ask an adult to help cut some slices of cheese. Add a slice to the top to make the band and half a cherry tomato for the buckle.

TOP TIP
Change the toppings to what you like and make different designs. You can use sweet or savory ingredients to make a big selection for your guests to choose from.

17

PARTY DECORATIONS

These crafts can help you create the perfect party atmosphere for you and your guests to enjoy. Make decorations, invitations, and more, all with a fairy tale twist!

How did Jack know how many beans his cow was worth? He used a cow-culator!

BEANSTALK TABLE DECORATIONS

"Jack and the Beanstalk" is a popular story, especially for children's plays. Jack trades his cow for some beans that magically grow into a very tall beanstalk. He climbs up the beanstalk, and when he reaches the clouds he discovers a giant's castle in the sky.

You Will Need:
- PAPER CUPS • NEWSPAPER
- MASKING TAPE • GLUE • GREEN PAINT
- PAINTBRUSH • GREEN TISSUE PAPER
- SMALL PLASTIC BAGS • RICE/DRIED BEANS

3. Fill some plastic bags with rice or dried beans and place them in the bottom of the cups.

1. Paint the paper cups in bright colors and leave to dry.

2. Twist sheets of newspaper into a beanstalk shape and hold in place with masking tape. Paint the stalks green and leave to dry.

4. Stick the beanstalk on top of the bags of beans or rice. Decorate with tissue paper bean pods, spirals, and leaves.

RAPUNZEL'S TOWER INVITATIONS

You Will Need:
- OLD BIRTHDAY CARD • CONSTRUCTION PAPER
- WHITE PAPER • SCISSORS
- COLORED MARKERS • GLUE STICK

The story of Rapunzel is hundreds of years old and has been told many different ways by different authors. A very early version seems to have been based on Saint Barbara. She was locked away in a tall tower by her father but, unlike the tales told today, her hair was definitely not long enough to help her escape.

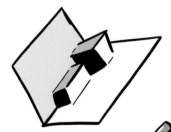

1. Fold the construction paper in half and cut it to make it the same size as your card. Fold the white paper in half and cut it so that it is slightly smaller than your construction paper.

2. Take the folded white sheet of paper and cut three lines as shown.

3. Push the cut-out sections inward and close the card to crease the sections. This will create a pop-up effect when the card is opened.

4. Decorate the pop-up sections to make them look like a tower and a roof.

TOP TIP
Use string to add a braid that hangs out of the middle of the window to look like Rapunzel's hair.

You are invited...

5. Stick each side of the white paper onto the construction paper you cut out earlier.

GOBLIN GOBLETS

Gulp down delicious homemade punch in style with these precious party cups.

You Will Need:

- CLEAR PLASTIC WINE GLASSES
- MULTI-COLORED PERMANENT MARKERS
- TIN FOIL
- GLUE STICK

1. Rip the tin foil into small pieces. Stick them onto the base and stem of the glass using the glue stick.

2. Draw and color in shapes on the bowl of the glass.

3. Go over the top of these shapes in a different color, drawing geometric lines to make the shapes look like gems.

PERFECT PUNCH RECIPE

With help from an adult, cut up lots of fruit (lemons, oranges, and strawberries work well) and put it in a large bowl. Add some orange juice, pineapple juice, and lemonade until the bowl is full. Squeeze in some fresh lime juice and mix it all together. Place some ice into your goblets and pour in your punch using a ladle.

REMEMBER

Do not decorate your goblets to the very top—you need to leave space so you can drink out of them safely.

FROG PRINCE CAKES

In the tale of the frog prince, an evil witch casts a spell on a prince and turns him into a frog. Only a kiss from a princess can reverse the magic. Could you be the one to break the spell?

You Will Need:
- SMALL SPONGE CAKE
- 2 TABLESPOONS OF READYMADE CHOCOLATE BUTTERCREAM FROSTING
- GREEN HARD CANDY
- PLASTIC BAG • ROLLING PIN
- YELLOW FONDANT ICING
- GREEN BAKING CUPS • SCISSORS

1. Break the cake up with your fingers until it is fine and crumbly.

2. Little by little, add some frosting to the crumbs and mix until it turns into a dough.

3. Place the candy in a plastic bag and crush it gently into a fine powder using the rolling pin.

Make some crowns from the fondant icing and press onto the heads of the frogs.

TOP TIP
Flatten out some baking cups and cut a "V" shape out of each of them. Put the cakes on top so it looks like frogs sitting on lily pads.

4. Mold the dough into frog shapes and dip into the crushed candy mix to give them a shimmery coat.

CRAFTY CREATIONS

Creating your own toys and decorations is so much fun. You can personalize them too, making each one truly unique. Follow these simple step-by-step instructions to create lots of fairy-tale-inspired crafts that are perfect as gifts but even better to keep.

FAIRY GARDEN

These tiny winged creatures are often hard to spot, so make your own and clip them to things around the house. Keep an eye on them—you never know what they might get up to when you're not looking!

You Will Need:
- WOODEN CLOTHESPINS • PAPER
- FLAT PLASTIC LID • CANDY WRAPPERS • MARKER • SCISSORS
- WHITE CRAFT GLUE

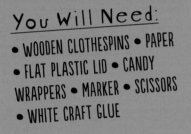

1. Draw and color in a fairy head and body.

2. Cut out the fairy and turn it over to color the other side.

3. Draw some wings onto the plastic lid and carefully cut them out.

4. Decorate the wings with torn-up pieces of candy wrappers and glue them on.

5. Glue the fairy body to one flat side of the pin and the wings to the other side. Leave to dry.

What do frog princes like to eat for lunch?

French flies!

THREE BEARS

Goldilocks stumbles across a house in the woods, but she does not realize that three bears live there. She eats their porridge, tries out their chairs, and sleeps in their beds. Once you have made your own bear family, see if you can make some of the other things in the story so you can act out this famous tale yourself.

You Will Need:
- SOCKS • FABRIC GLUE • SCISSORS
- TOY STUFFING OR SCRAP FABRIC
- ELASTIC BANDS • FELT
- PERMANENT MARKER

1. Fill the sock with the toy stuffing and stuff the remainder of the sock inside itself so no stuffing escapes.

TOP TIP
Follow the steps twice more so that you make all three bears—but make sure you use socks of different sizes so that the bears are different sizes, too.

2. Loosely wrap the elastic band around the top to make the head.

3. Tightly wrap more elastic bands to make four small balls. These will be the hands and feet.

4. Cut out ears and a face from the felt and stick them onto the bear's head.

5. Use the permanent marker to draw details on the face, such as eyes, a nose, and a mouth.

GIANT'S LEGS

"Fee-fi-fo-fum" is the traditional call from the giant in the story "Jack and the Beanstalk." Surprise your guests by making a giant to greet them at your party!

You Will Need:
- 2 COAT HANGERS • WHITE PLASTIC BAGS
- THIN CARDSTOCK • TAPE • BLUE PAINT
- SCISSORS • PERMANENT MARKER

1. Paint lots of sheets of cardstock blue on both sides and leave to dry before folding back and forth.

2. Stick the sheets of folded cardstock together using tape. Join enough pieces together so they reach the ceiling. Make two strips.

3. Tape each of these long strips onto a hanger to make the giant's legs.

4. Scrunch up some plastic bags and fix them to each hanger to hide them and make them look like clouds.

TOP TIP
Make two more hangers to go on either side of the legs as arms. Hook them all onto a curtain pole to make your giant.

5. Make some shoes using more of the cardstock, drawing on details with permanent marker. Stick them onto the end of the legs. If there's time, you could also make a pair of arms.

ENCHANTED CASTLE SNOW GLOBE

You Will Need:
- JAM JAR AND LID • GLITTER
- WATER • FLAT PLASTIC LID
- SCISSORS • PERMANENT MARKERS
- GLUE • RED AND GREEN TISSUE PAPER
- MODELING CLAY

In the story of Sleeping Beauty, the princess falls into a deep sleep as soon as she pricks her finger on a spinning wheel. The whole castle falls under the spell too, falling asleep where they stand, leaving the castle still and overgrown with plants for many years. Make your own enchanted castle that you can shake. Do you think you can wake up everyone inside?

3. Press the castle into the clay, making sure it is very secure.

1. Press some modeling clay onto the inside of the jam jar lid.

2. Cut out a castle shape from a plastic lid and color using the permanent markers.

4. Fill the jar with water and glitter and carefully screw on the lid.

5. Turn the jar over and cover the lid with green tissue paper and glue to make overgrown vines. Use red tissue paper to make roses.

STORY MEMORY BOOK

All great stories start with "Once upon a time," but what happens after that is up to you! Make your own book and fill it with old pictures and notes on what adventures you have been on. What will be your favorite chapter?

You Will Need:
- PAPER • HOLE PUNCH • STRING
- THICK CARDBOARD • WRAPPING PAPER • WHITE CRAFT GLUE

1. Pile the papers on top of each other and make some holes using the hole punch. Feed the string through the holes to bind the pages together. Remember to tie the string at both ends so that it does not come loose.

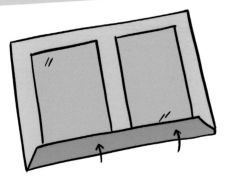

2. Make a cover from thick cardboard that is slightly bigger than the pages of the book. Glue the cardboard onto the wrapping paper. Fold the cover over and glue the edges.

3. Put glue in the middle of the pages and two bits of cardboard and place the pages inside the cover. Let dry.

4. Decorate the cover with cardboard corners and put a sign in the middle to add the title of your story.

FAIRY LIGHTS

You won't need to find fairy dust to make these fairies sparkle in the dark—these magical creatures light up using LED lights. If you don't have any LED lights, you can hang your fairies in the window and watch them catch the sunlight.

You Will Need:
- PLASTIC BOTTLES AND LIDS • TAPE
- SCISSORS • LED LIGHTS
- CANDY WRAPPERS/SHINY PAPER
- PERMANENT MARKER

1. Cut your bottles in half and cover the edges with tape to make sure there are no sharp bits.

2. Place the bulb onto the neck of the bottle and fix the wire in place using tape. Don't cover the bulb.

3. Decorate the bottle with layers of candy wrappers or shiny paper, fixing them in place with tape.

4. Draw a face on the bottle lid with the permanent marker and add candy wrappers or shiny paper for hair. Make some wings from the bottom of the cut bottle. Cover the edges with tape and decorate.

5. Make sure all fairy bottles are attached securely to the wire, then hang them up and enjoy the sparkle!

MAGIC MIRROR

The evil queen in "Snow White" has her very own enchanted mirror. It tells her who is the fairest in the land when she looks into it and says the magic spell. What will yours say to you?

You Will Need:
- CARDBOARD • NEWSPAPER • MASKING TAPE • WHITE CRAFT GLUE • TIN FOIL • SCISSORS • PAINT • PAINTBRUSH

1. Cut out a mirror shape and a border using the cardboard.

2. Scrunch up shapes made from newspaper and tape them to the mirror to make the face.

3. Spread a thin layer of glue over the mirror and shapes. Cover them with the tin foil.

4. Gently press down on the tin foil so it reveals the face.

5. Stick on the border and paint any bare cardboard.

MINI KINGDOMS

Each fairy story is based in a different realm of a magical kingdom. Bring all the stories together by making mini story boxes filled with your favorite characters. They are stackable so you can create a whole wall of make-believe that you have bought to life.

You Will Need:

• SMALL BOXES (OLD SHOE BOXES ARE PERFECT) • PAPER • CARDBOARD
• PENS • SCISSORS • GLUE STICK

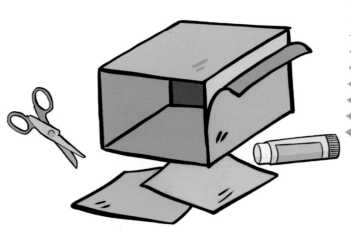

1. Cover the box in one color by cutting the paper to the size of the sides and gluing it in place.

TOP TIP

If you are not confident in drawing the characters for your story boxes, look through any magazines you have and cut out characters from there. You could also print some from a computer.

2. Draw the scenery and characters onto the paper and cardboard. When you cut them out, remember to leave tabs on so that you can stick them in place.

3. Stick them all in place using the glue stick. If you want to make some movable, stick them onto a thin cardboard base instead.

What Story?

In one box, you can place the tall beanstalk that reaches the giant's home in the clouds. In another, you can set an underwater scene where a little mermaid can swim around. Create magical forests where you can hide trolls in the trees or discover a witch's gingerbread house. And don't forget to make a big castle for all your knights to live in before they ride off to visit faraway lands! If you're stuck and can't think of any more ideas, just open your favorite collection of fairy tales and use the stories as inspiration.

FAIRY PUZZLE

CAN YOU FIND THE ANSWERS TO THESE QUESTIONS?

1. How many stars can you find in the picture?

2. Where is the gnome hiding?

3. Which is the odd unicorn out?

4. How many rubies can you spot?

A

B

C

D